Ice Cream CLUB

Wrriten by

Dr. Hoot

Published in 2025 by Skooler Books

Ice Cream Club

Skooler Books

ISBN:9789354695056

Dedicated to

MY MOM

ice cream
ice cream

Yum Yum Yum

eating it is so much FUN...

It comes in cone

it comes in cup

scoop it down

and lick it up.

slurp slurp

lick lick

slurp

lick

slick

in the sun it melts so Quick.

ice cream
ice cream

in the
sun
it melts
so
Quick.

ice cream
ice cream

Yum Yum Yum

cold and tasty

sweet

and

fun..

So,

Grab a spoon and
come with me.
we will find how
they can be !

pink
ice cream
is soft
and sweet

white

is cool

and

yellow

is

treat.

one scoop

two scoop

three scoop

cream

i really really love ice cream.

More from the Series

www.ingramcontent.com/pod-product-compliance
Ingram Content Group UK Ltd.
Pitfield, Milton Keynes, MK11 3LW, UK
UKHW061433190726
13845UKWH00021B/172
* 9 7 8 9 3 5 4 6 9 5 0 5 6 *